THE KEY TO ART

THE KEY TO ART
FROM ROMANTICISM
TO IMPRESSIONISM

Carlos Reyero
Professor of Art History

Lerner Publications Company ♦ Minneapolis

The publisher wishes to thank Dale Haworth, Professor of
Art History, Carleton College, for his assistance in the
preparation of this book.

Words that appear in **bold** type are listed in the glossary.

This edition published 1990
by Lerner Publications Company
241 First Avenue North, Minneapolis, Minnesota 55401, USA

In association with David Bateman Ltd.
32-34 View Road, Glenfield, Auckland, New Zealand

LIBRARY OF CONGRESS CATALOGING-IN-PUBLICATION DATA

Reyero, Carlos.
 [Del romanticismo al impresionismo. English]
 The key to art from romanticism to impressionism /
Carlos Reyero.
 p. cm.—(The Key to art)
 Translation of: Del romanticismo al impresionismo.
 "In association with David Bateman Ltd. ... Glenfield,
Auckland, New Zealand"—T.p. verso.
 "A David Bateman book"—T.p. verso.
 Includes index.
 ISBN 0-8225-2058-3
 ISBN 0-8225-2061-3 (pbk.)
 1. Art, Modern—19th century—Themes, motives—Juvenile
literature. I. Title. II. Series.
N6450.R4513 1990
709.03'4—dc20   89-34982
                                                 CIP
                                                 AC

A David Bateman Book

Printed in Spain
Bound in USA by Muscle Bound Bindery
1 2 3 4 5 6 7 8 9 10 99 98 97 96 95 94 93 92 91 90

INTRODUCTION

Evaluation, Tendencies, and Terminology

The idea that no distinct artistic style emerged during the 19th century was a common belief during that period and one that still persists today. Although it is true that most artistic forms used during the 19th century are no different from those of other periods, the words *19th century* do have a meaning that is much wider than a mere reference to time.

CHARLES GARNIER. Great Stairway at the Opera. 1860-64. Paris. The Opera in Paris is an important work that typifies the architecture of the 19th century. The building is an outstanding example of the architecture of the Second Empire. Perfectly situated on its surrounding square of land, it was a point of reference for Parisian town planning. It has all of the elements of Eclectic Classicism, and its sumptuous interior shows the taste of the powerful middle class for the grandiose and overpowering. Because of its luxurious and exaggerated detail, it has an unequalled capacity to surprise.

MAP

Paris is considered to have been the most important artistic center of the 19th century. It was receptive to new ideas and served as a reference point for the rest of Europe in all art forms throughout the century. But there were also other artistic centers where new ideas sprang up before or at the same time as those in France. Classical art influenced much 19th-century art. Rome (which is known for its Classical art) exercised an artistic power over cities such as Paris and Venice. Important 19th-century art was also created in London, Berlin, Vienna, Munich, Budapest, Brussels, as well as the artistic centers of Russia, Spain, and Portugal. Eventually, art was no longer exclusively European: The United States started producing its own art, which, in turn, had some influence on Europe. Nineteenth-century European art was also influenced, stylistically and iconographically, by cultures from the Near and Far East.

1. St. Petersburg
2. Berlin
3. Dresden
4. Vienna
5. Munich
6. Copenhagen
7. Venice
8. Florence
9. Rome
10. Barcelona
11. Madrid
12. Lisbon
13. Paris
14. London
15. Brussels

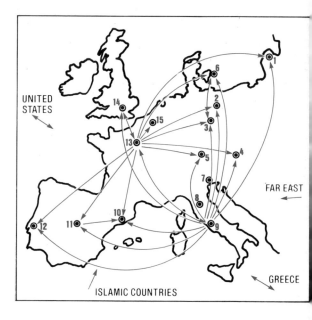

In some way, the words *19th century* serve to unify what some art historians have tried very hard to put into categories. These historians are referring to artistic tendencies whose development can be traced from the end of the 18th century to the end of the 19th century.

4

**FREDERICK-AUGUSTE
BARTHOLDI.** *Liberty
Enlightening the World.*
1884. New York.
Public works of architec-
ture or sculpture have often
become symbols of towns,
cities, and even whole
nations. It is almost always
a building or a monument
from the 19th century that
has been adopted as a symbol. The Statue of Liberty,
which the government of
the French Republic gave
to the United States of
America, is one of the most
significant of these works.
It was conceived as a modern lighthouse (with struc-
tural supports created
by Gustave Eiffel, who
designed the Eiffel Tower in
Paris), but Bartholdi's
colossal statue has become
more than a utilitarian
work—it has become a very
symbolic sculpture.

CASPAR DAVID FRIEDRICH. *Two Men Contemplating the Moon.* 1819. Gemäldegalerie, Dresden.

Many Romantic paintings have a meaning conceived by the artist or suggested by his or her contemporaries, but the interpretation of a painting is continually changing. People have tried to find political, religious, and artistic symbolism in this painting, in which much of the expression appears through the forces of nature. The two figures— almost certainly

Romanticism was an historical attitude toward life and art in general that started at the end of the 18th century in Europe and England. It is difficult to define the term in a way that would be valid for all the works of art that could be called Romantic. The term *Romantic* was used in England as early as the 17th century. It was not until the end of the 18th century, though, that it began to be used to refer to short stories and novels of a "fantasy" nature and became a recognized term. The term would certainly not have been applied to a particular period or to a particular style if French art historians had not begun using it to compare the work of certain artists. From then on, people began to speak of a Romantic school—or at least of Romantic artists—in both literature and the visual arts.

However, there was never a concrete statement

of principles that established a starting point to separate Romanticism from other contemporary movements. Therefore, any definition of Romanticism is likely to include ambiguity and diversity. Both individual and historical aspects must be considered when defining Romantic works. Each person is a unique spectator of the world and works of art result from each individual's particular vision. "No two people have ever read the same book nor seen the same painting," said Preault, a 19th-century sculptor.

Subjectivity—an artist's personal view—is the

key to Romantic diversity. This key opens two doors. One door projects the individual into the outside world—dark, abysmal, violent, and fantastic—where nature appears to have a life of its own and the irrational is more powerful than the rational. The second door opens to a world where nature and the external world are excluded and there is a proclamation of the self, including an investigation of desires, dreams and nightmares, magic, and religious expression.

A sense of history is also fundamental to Romanticism. Romantic art embodies the realization that time is passing very quickly. It also shows a desire to recapture the past. This nostalgia was

the artist himself and a pupil—stand close together, contemplating something far from human understanding, as if they were undergoing a mystical experience.

FRANCISCO DE PAULA VAN HALEN. *The Running of the Bulls in Picturesque and Artistic Spain.*
One of the most revealing signs of Romantic feeling was the interest in cultures outside of the Western world. Anything Islamic held a particular attraction This applies to the Romantic vision of Spain both from within and from outside its borders. Spain's dancers, fiestas, macho men, common country folk, and, above all, Spanish-Muslim monuments such as the Alhambra (palace of the Moorish kings) were constantly used as symbols of Spain. The cities of Seville and Granada helped evoke a sensual and festive world.

JENARO PÉREZ VILLAAMIL. *The Castle of Gaucín.* **Museo de Bellas Artes, Granada.** *Ravines in the Alpujarras.* **Colegio de Santamarca, Madrid.**

An interest in historical styles runs parallel to the enjoyment of the architectural glories of the past. This is why medieval monuments, Islamic and Christian, are so often depicted in drawings and engravings. Such works portray a picturesque fantasy suggested by some ruin or monument. They also reveal a desire to know and to restore the ruin or monument. Villaamil, one of Spain's best landscape artists during the first half of the 19th century, painted vistas representative of the wide and theatrical Romantic "way of seeing."

the source of emotions and the basis of most art forms of the time.

Romanticism did not follow **Neoclassicism,** as some other historical movements did. Rather there was a gradual change during the first decades of the 19th century. It is difficult to know if this process of change was a conscious or an unconscious movement, if it was a response to a philosophy with stated aims or if it was simply a normal evolution. One could argue in support of either theory.

It is valid to use the term *Eclecticism* to classify most of the artistic creations of the 19th century. **Eclecticism** is not a burst of new ideas, but a blend of elements drawn from various sources. A very strong and widespread artistic movement, Eclecticism was already well known at the start of the century.

According to Eclectic philosophy, there were neither Classical nor Romantic artists. There were only good artists and bad artists, and the distinction between the two types seemed perfectly clear. Eclecticism endorsed the idea that order and progress were unchanging values—values higher than those of society and art. Eclectic artists felt that by being open to all influences they could arrive at a "happy medium" and create truth and beauty.

Traditionally, Eclecticism was not very highly esteemed. It was considered pompous, dull, superficial, false, and lacking in originality. In the middle of the century, such criticism came from the Realists—those who aspired to offer a true, impartial, and objective view of the real world, based on careful observation of contemporary life. **Realism** spread throughout Europe and America. "Let us be savage," said French novelist

WILLIAM BOUGUEREAU. *Cupid.* **c. 1895. Private Collection.**
The emergence of Realism did not result in a crisis in academic Eclecticism—at least insofar as official recognition and popularity of the artists were concerned. Eclecticism was fed basically by Raphael and Ingres. Bouguereau was the main practitioner of this style, which some critics called false and showy. In his paintings, he used religion or mythology as a theme, and his works are characterized by uniform and pearly surfaces. They also include fine details.

9

CONSTANTIN MEUNIER. *The Forge*. Musée d'Art, Antwerp. One of the most powerful forces of Realism was the replacement of the epics of ancient times with every-day events. Rather than portraying heroism, Realist artists tried to give dignity to common tasks. Unlike the Romantics, the Realists depicted things as they were.

Gustave Flaubert. "Let us pour strong liquor ove this century of sugary water. Let us drown th bourgeoisie in strong liquor until their snout burn and they scream with pain." Criticism of th conventional is a vital part of Realism. Howeve to suppose that Realism produced an exact refle tion of reality is an oversimplification. Reality ca never be duplicated, and an artist's perception o it is never pure.

The move toward recording contemporary lif was unstoppable. Recording one instant in th contemporary world became part of the visua philosophy of **Impressionism,** the movemen that succeeded Realism. Thus, Impressionisn appears as the reduction of Realism to an instan to an artist's "impression" of a precise momen Impressionists used details to create a sensor impression rather than a social message, whicl was important in the works of many Realists.

Another style that began in the middle of the 9th century is **Aestheticism.** Considered to be he opposite of Realism, Aestheticism reveals an bsessive preoccupation with beauty. Aestheti-ism raises beauty to the category of an end in self, ignoring concerns for morality in art. Exam-les of the extreme use of the Aesthetic can be und in the castles of Ludwig II of Bavaria.

Near the end of the century, **Symbolism** was nother reaction against Realism. The Symbol-ts were obsessed with two different subjects: ex and spirituality. They wanted to express the nmaterial, the ideal, by using sensuous repre-entations, and they exalted the mysterious.

FORD MADOX BROWN. *Toil.* 1852-65. Manchester Art Gallery, Manchester. This picture is of special interest because of its ico-nography and formal treat-ment of theme. It illustrates the elevation of manual labor, but with a touch of Symbolism. The apparent casualness of the scene is not really convincing. The painter makes it clear that setting the scene in the full summer sun was a deliber-ate choice and was meant to emphasize the serious-ness of the content of the picture. The Realists often used a representational style that the 19th century was reluctant to abandon.

rtists and Society in the 19th Century

R omantic artists are often described as ado-lescent, melancholy, and unstable. They do not "reproduce" nature, but interpret . The Romantic artist is usually portrayed as an solated genius.

The professional status of the artist in the 19th entury depended a great deal on the official

GUSTAVE MOREAU.
The Apparition. 1874-76.
Musée Moreau, Paris.

A recurrent theme used by Symbolists is *la femme fatalè*. This attraction toward woman is mixed with horror and a pleasure in self-destruction. Three typical portrayals of this theme include: woman as a vampire or as an angel of death; woman as a hybrid creature, particularly the Sphinx; and woman as a complex, gorgeous, and mysterious heroine, like Helen of Troy or Cleopatra. The superhuman Salome shown here is a dreamlike figure. She acts with indifference and irresponsibility— insensitive to whatever happens. She is shown, almost nude, before a splendid backdrop of a golden castle. She is draped in shining lace and drips with blood, balsam, and incense. John the Baptist's head, bathed in light, forces the terrified Salome to look at it, though she longs to push it away.

French Academy. That institution awarded ce[r]tificates which guaranteed the professional qua[l]ifications of artists and allowed them to practic[e] as professionals. Recognized artists could expec[t] to occupy important social positions, practice [a] second profession such as teaching, and obtai[n] state commissions (payments for specific work[s] of art).

In the 19th century, a work of art was consid[]ered from two distinct points of view: private an[d] public. After the French Revolution, art—as a[ll] other aspects of life—could not avoid the swing[s] of politics. Art occupied a prominent position i[n] a society that was undergoing sudden transfor[]mations. Never before had art, either public o[r]

12

rivate, been so subject to social ideas as during
his century.

In general, two attitudes were revealed. The
pper class favored the art of Eclecticism. The
orking class, on the other hand, favored the
ealists, who were viewed as social reporters. The
hop windows for the **fine arts** were the official
lons and the independent exhibitions. Artists
ere subjected, as seldom before, to public opin-
n. Critics became primary indicators of the
ocial structure that ruled the behavior and even
he artistic forms of the time. Juries were formed
o decide which artists could exhibit their work
the official salons. These juries often became
rannical about whose work was acceptable and
hose was not. There was so much protest about
he juries' decisions that independent exhibitions
ere formed. An example of an independent exhi-
tion was the one established by Gustave Courbet
1855. It was a deliberate move to argue against
he officially sanctioned salons. In 1863, the offi-
al salon refused so many entrants that a "Salon
s Refuses" was established to show the work of
hose artists whose work had been rejected. The
aternalistic attitude of the state toward art began
o disintegrate, and by the 1870s the Impres-
onists were showing in private galleries.

During the last third of the 19th century, some
rtists tried to reestablish the role of craftspeople
the arts, particularly by broadening the defini-
on of art to include the decorative arts. This
ovement was also an attempt to interest the
iddle class and the rapidly expanding indus-
ies in a protest against what was considered rou-
ne and trivial.

PHILIPP OTTO RUNGE.
Self-Portrait. **1802.**
Kunsthalle, Hamburg.
In this self-portrait, Runge
shows himself as a young
man with a strange look in
his eyes and the melan-
choly features of someone
who has probed deeply
into the darkest corners of
his being. In his solitude,
he seems to belong to
another world and to have
no need to adorn himself—
as happened in previous
periods—with all the trap-
pings of a society that he
dared to despise. He gazes
at us, slightly challenging
but not quite secure—
somewhat subdued by the
overwhelming forces of
creation.

JERÓNIMO SUÑOL.
Dante. **1864. Museum of
Modern Art, Barcelona.**
National fine arts exhibitions were, for many artists, a means of gaining the public acclaim that would allow them to develop their art. This work won second prize in such an exhibition. Dante, a favorite subject of the Romantics, is treated here with a serenity and solidity that recall Neoclassicism. The sculpture's simplicity is more the result of restraint than of a wish to present the theme in a new way. Spanish sculpture soon moved from this style to more ostentatious work.

TOWN PLANNING

The Industrial Revolution had sparked a undreamed-of growth of cities. It becan vital to expand the narrow limits of th old city center, to establish methods of rapid communication, and to try to balance the need fo housing and the growth of the economy. Th function-versus-form debate was to shape muc town planning and architecture of the 19t century.

People realized that the number and placement
: important buildings established a city's own
)ecial personality and was thus important from
political and prestige point of view. Socially, the
)th-century city is composed of various quar-
rs, each of which is defined within its street plan.
ouses formed a part of this plan, and their
cades, or fronts, gave the plan a unified appear-
ice.

The ideas of some planners, known as "uto-
an urban planners," were seldom put into prac-
ce. Their plans had two things in common. First,
iey included new centers, or downtown areas,
iat would keep the benefits of the new industri-
ization but still offer opportunities for new
)cial relationships. Communal living spaces
ere to be created in which each individual and
:tivity formed part of an economic system, but
iese spaces were to be located away from all the
nsions of manufacturing and commerce. Sec-
id, these plans were designed to put older build-
gs to new use. For example, a baroque palace
rved as the basis for the design of a community
.ilding.

**GEORGES
HAUSSMANN. *Plan of
Paris*. 1853-69.**
The idea of reshaping Paris
arose more from a desire
for publicity than from a
need to practice modern
town planning. Old build-
ings like Notre Dame and
contemporary ones such as
the Opera were more easily
admired after the demoli-
tion of nearby housing.
Boulevards and avenues
were opened not only to
clear up the inner city, but
also to cross the whole city
with splendid new arterial
roads and tempt visitors
into shops and theaters.
In the redesign of the city,
ease of access was more
important than architec-
ture, but the addition of
many gardens and trees
helped turn Paris into a
pleasant city.

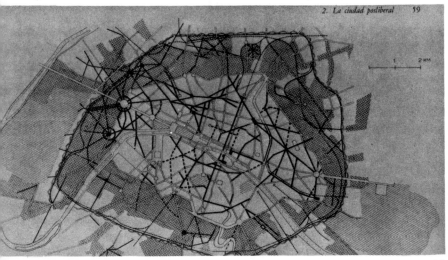

2. La ciudad postliberal   59

CHARLES FOURIER.
Plan of a Community Residence. 1822.
This plan envisioned a single building as the home for a community of some 1,500 people of all ages. It was meant to replace the disorder and filth of miserable slums. Structurally, the building bears an extraordinary resemblance to royal Baroque palaces, an example of Fourier's wish to put the luxurious buildings of the past to new uses.

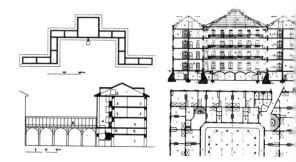

The growth of European and American citie was governed by two opposing principles: respe for private property and the urgent need for cor trol of sanitation and hygiene. In population London was the largest city in 19th-centur Europe. Miserable slums coexisted alongsid exquisite blocks of buildings in green ope

Plan of the "Ring" of Vienna. 1859-72.
A great circular road, the Ringstrasse, was built around old Vienna. The redesigned city is one of the finest combinations of 19th-century aesthetic Eclecticism and town planning. The Neoclassic parliament building, the Gothic city hall, the town theater in Italian style, and the French-influenced university are the main buildings of Vienna that appeared on the Ring. Together with the Opera, they form a unique mixture of Classical urban tradition, 19th-century style, and the demands of the modern world.

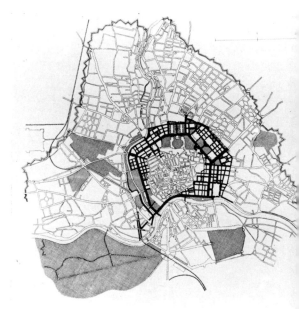

16

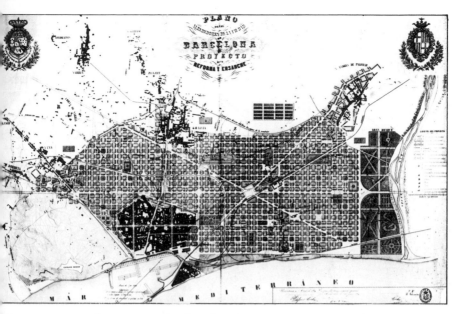

ILDEFONSO CERDÁ.
Plan for the Reform and Expansion of Barcelona.
1860.

A royal decree on July 8, 1860, gave approval for the expansion of Barcelona. In a competition the town council gave first prize to a plan for a fan-shaped expansion that used the old city as its base and had main arteries converge on it. Cerdá, whose proposal we see here, designed a network of streets parallel and vertical to the sea, on which would be superimposed two great diagonal roads. The plan showed extraordinary attention to social considerations and services and to great, wide streets. Cerdá's *General Theory of Town Planning* (1867) is one of the earliest studies of modern town plans.

spaces. Paris claimed to be the most beautiful capital in Europe, and it reflected the prestige of all of France. Certain buildings were recognized as important monuments and were the focus of avenues and tree-lined boulevards set up to cross the city. Paris was created by annexing villages and renovating the old center. In other cities, the old historic centers were kept intact. For example, in Vienna, expansion took place around a circular road, and in Barcelona, a grid crossed by diagonals was cleverly blended with the old city.

ARCHITECTURE

Art historians have explained the evolution of 19th-century architecture as a constant interplay between the imitation of well-established forms (called **historicism,** Eclecticism, or Beaux Arts academicism) and the requirements of structure, space, and aesthetics imposed by new materials and new construction methods.

A feeling for the **picturesque** is shown in much of the architecture of the time. The picturesque is not a style but a point of view or a feeling. It should be thought of as the starting point of the architectural transformation that occurred during the 19th century. The picturesque included asymmetrical plans, a search for effects that contrasted surprisingly with nature, and, above all, exotic design. Use of these elements resulted in an emergence of forms selected from many different Western styles (particularly **Gothic**), from the Far East (India and China), or from local rustic tradition.

The interest in historical styles other than those of Greece and Italy started with the purely picturesque. Gradually, however, an interest in archaeological correctness (historicism) arose, and a true "revival" spirit was finally adopted by architects. The architect had the freedom to build according to one style or another but still comply with well-established formal rules of the past. When one speaks of Neoclassical or Neo-Gothic architecture, the reference is strictly in terms of

19

**JOHN NASH. Royal
Pavilion. 1815-23.
Brighton.**
Nash was an Eclectic who
showed a sensitivity for the
picturesque, as seen in this
sumptuously decorated
building. He produced
something magical and
frivolous with a capricious
mixture of Chinese,
Islamic, Byzantine, and
Indian styles. However, the
distribution and use of
space within the building
is strictly controlled. An
important novelty was the
use of cast iron as an architectural element, although
it is hidden beneath the
exotic exterior.

form and rarely in terms of function or materia
The term *historicism* basically has only a theoret
ical meaning. The choice of a distinct historica
style did not indicate the ultimate use to which
the building would be put. For example, the Clas
sical style was not always used just for publi
buildings or the Gothic just for religious build
ings. Rather, the adaptation of traditional build
ing and a new investigation into past styles wer
blended with a gradual use of new materials an
modern requirements.

The Gothic style became particularly impor
tant during the 19th century. The first example
of Neo-Gothic architecture appeared at the en
of the 18th century. Many picturesque countr
houses were built throughout England. Flirtin
with the Middle Ages was common among th
Romantics. However, the rediscovery of th
Gothic style carried new connotations. First, i

CHARLES BARRY and AUGUST PUGIN. Houses of Parliament. 1836-67. London.
A superficial study of the Houses of Parliament might lead one to conclude that it is a capricious and picturesque building, but only the unequal towers placed asymmetrically and its site next to the Thames River really have those characteristics. This is a building constructed in a conventional way, with two axes crossing in the center and a tower raised over the crossing. It is a balanced and logical building, but one that is modeled after the Gothic period rather than the Neoclassical.

Germany, England, and France, Gothic architecture became identified with nationalism. Second, Gothic style became associated with religious architecture. This implied both a rediscovery of the Gothic style as an expression of medieval spiritual values and a link between form and function. It meant, too, that the Gothic style became an alternative to the Classical. As the Gothic style developed throughout the century, what could have been considered picturesque frivolities instead became academic works based on archaeology. Because the choice of Gothic as a style was sometimes dictated by the cost of the work, some distortion of historical accuracy often occurred. Gothic architecture became a well-documented system that allowed an architect to express any symbolic function.

During the second half of the 19th century, the position of Gothic style was strengthened by two

EUGÈNE-EMMANUEL VIOLLET-LE-DUC. Illustration from *Le Dictionnaire Raisonné de l'Architecture Française*. 1854-64. Viollet-le-Duc restored Notre Dame Çathedral in Paris, the Cluniac Abbey at Vezelay, and some of the other great French medieval monuments. In addition, he designed a number of churches, all of which show his archaeological interest. Although he was a great theoretical architect, his major reputation came from his dictionary, which provided a thorough understanding of Gothic architecture.

new and seemingly contradictory influence that linked Romantic architecture to the more functional works at the end of the century. The first of these influences was Aestheticism. John Ruskin was its main defender, and through his writings—especially *Seven Lamps of Architectur*

FRANCISCO JAREÑO. National Library. 1865. Madrid. The completion of the Palace of Libraries and Museums was the most important architectural achievement in 19th-century Madrid. The building has a careful balance of academic and Eclectic elements, with a Greek facade on the second story of the Museum of Archaeology, shown here. The plan of

he building is almost
quare, with two cross-
haped galleries and four
ery traditional courtyards.

There is also an early use
of cast iron in the building.
This structure presents an
honest use of materials,

such as brick and stone,
with no attempt to disguise
or twist them to fit a
chosen style.

23

(1849) and *The Stones of Venice* (1851-1853)—h
argued that Gothic was the only style that ha
not been debased and degraded in the face of th
new industrial civilization. He also promote
craftsmanship, emotion, and good taste rathe
than the products of utilitarian mass productior

**JOSEPH PAXTON.
Crystal Palace. 1850-51.
London.**
The first Universal Exhibition took place in London
in 1851. After an international competition in which
all building plans submit-
ted were rejected, the exhibition organizers drew up
their own rather conserva-
tive plans. Paxton, well
known for his designs of
greenhouses, then pro-
duced a set of plans that
was speedily adopted.
Because of his design, this
building was completed
quickly and at low cost.
Paxton combined the new
techniques of cast-iron
construction (using pre-
fabricated, mass-produced
units) with a traditional
treatment of decorative features and the basilica-like
aspect of the building. But
the real achievement was
the creation of a large, well-
lit space that appeared to be
almost unlimited; it was
marvelled at by all visitors.

Ruskin emphasized ornamental and visual val
ues, sensitivity to materials, colors, and textures
simplicity of construction, and the integration o
other art forms such as sculpture and painting
He stressed the need for additional decoration t
enrich a building without hiding its basic struc
ture. He also believed that Gothic style should b
adapted to new materials and, above all, to a mod
ern, functional approach that would form th
basis of a new architecture.

The second influence on the Gothic style deal
with the techniques of building. Eugène
Emmanuel Viollet-de-Duc did the most to lin
Gothic methods of building to the 19th centur
His use of the Gothic style on existing building
was the real beginning of modern architecture.

Along with an interest in various Gothic style
throughout the century, the Classical styles o
ancient Greece and Rome also contributed to var
iations of Eclecticism. One variation, called Beau:
Arts Eclecticism, received its name from the fac
that its practitioners came from the School o

24

Beaux Arts in Paris. This school had great prestige in both Europe and the United States during the second half of the 19th century.

The key to understanding 19th-century Eclecticism lies in recognizing that an architectural work is a combination of already-accepted styles. An architect selects and uses these styles according to technical and artistic requirements. Depending upon the imagination of the architect and the purposes of a work, the results could vary from masterpieces to the most unexpected combinations possible. Formal, symmetrical design—with regular cross sections and straight lines—often coexisted alongside more capricious and irregu-

lar design derived from the picturesque. But this practice was more common in England than in other European countries.

The history of 19th-century architecture is not just a debate about the reinterpretation of past styles. However, this was an important factor at the time, and modern art historians still find it worthy of study. Also involved were the direct consequences of the Industrial Revolution, new construction methods inspired by the use of new

HENRI LABROUSTE. Reading Room of the National Library. 1857-67. Paris.
This work is one of the first that attempted to combine the new architectural possibilities opened up by cast iron with the principles of international Eclecticism. Incorporated into a series of older buildings, the reading room achieves its functional purpose of providing a well-lit, open space. Its slender cast-iron columns support domes of **terracotta** and glass. Despite this use of modern materials, however, the room has a traditional 19th-century look. It demonstrates that new materials did not necessarily bring about a completely new style. Instead, they were incorporated into earlier, well-known architectural forms. A truly new style of architecture was yet to come.

GIUSEPPE MENGONI. Gallery of Victor Emmanuel II. 1865-75. Milan.

It has been said that today's temples—shopping malls and supermarkets, railway stations and airports—are dedicated to commerce and communications. The arcade, or covered walkway, was typical of the 19th century and is where one often finds examples of historical forms adapted to new materials and new methods of construction.

materials, and the need to respond to requirements that had never before been met.

The parts of buildings made of iron, such as columns and girders, had been used in traditional architecture since ancient times. But it was not until **cast iron** became available that it was widely used in buildings. Iron is fireproof, relatively durable, and easily shaped. Utilitarian structures such as bridges were the first in which iron was substituted completely for masonry—without any attempt to disguise the ironwork. The first such bridge in the world was opened on New Year's Day, 1781, at Ironbridge, England. By the mid-19th century, such works were considered practical engineering solutions, unconnected with "architecture." Today those works are viewed as highly important because they led to other developments. The split between engineers and architects continued throughout the century, and professionals from both areas had to be employed n a project to supply the needed technical and rtistic expertise.

By the middle of the century, buildings relying ntirely on load-bearing iron or steel began to ppear. Most such buildings were markets, train tations, and greenhouses. Often, particularly in rain stations, their external appearance was disuised to hide the real function of the building.

Around the middle of the century, a new style f cast-iron buildings emerged as the usefulness f cast iron came to be appreciated. This style vas based on the possibility that a building could e erected with very slim metal columns, and it vould then have a great amount of free internal pace. Large exhibition halls built with cast iron reflect the taste of the century for ever-larger, ver-taller buildings. Use of the style declined fter it became apparent that cast iron was not quite so durable as had once been believed.

The introduction of cast iron into Eclectic archiecture posed problems, and it never became a rincipal building material. However, it was dapted to new needs and became integrated into unctional structures.

This arcade in Milan is in the shape of a cross with an octagonal space at the intersection of the arms. One cannot help but be impressed by its size and by the heavy use of ornate detail.

GUSTAVE EIFFEL. Eiffel Tower. 1887-89. Paris. Although this tower is now considered one of the masterpieces of the 19th century, it displeased the majority of people at the time it was erected. The tower was constructed completely with prefabricated iron parts. From a strictly functional point of view, it is not a building, but from its beginning as a structure for the Universal Exhibition of 1889, it has become the most important symbol of the city of Paris. For the first time—and this is its real importance—so-called iron architecture, which had been used previously only as a hidden framework, was used in a provocative and defiant way. Cast iron was used with no attempt to disguise it.

SCULPTURE

FRANÇOIS RUDE. *The Marseillaise*. **1835-36. Paris.**

This relief sculpture on the Arc de Triomphe—commonly known as *The Marseillaise*—represents volunteers departing for a 1792 war. Rivalry among artists working on the arch caused Rude's work to be restricted to this one sculpture, and it is the only one on the monument that shows inspiration and spirit. There are obvious references to Neoclassicism in the heroic nudes, but it is the enraged and explosive cry of the winged figure that transmits a more dominant expression of Romanticism. A revolutionary anthem, captured in stone, displays movement and dynamism.

There are two problems to be considered when analyzing 19th-century sculpture: 1) how to identify and define the formal and thematic elements, which stemmed from the classical tradition but were influenced by 19th-century tendencies; and 2) how to recognize changes in the traditional ideas about sculpture. Historically, sculpture had always been regarded as inferior to architecture and painting. Now, however, the 19th century is seen as a golden age of sculpture.

There is a strong Romantic spirit in 19th-century sculpture. Although painters repeatedly claimed that sculpture was incapable of expressing such a spirit, sculptors tried to show that their creations were a response to the same revolutionary cry as those of painters. The sculpture of the time does exhibit a conscious Romantic feeling, and in some cases, this feeling is recognizable in theme or form. It is impossible to lay down rules for this style, to compare works, or to define time periods when Romantic sculpture flourished. Nevertheless, many artists from different countries—generally classified as Classical artists—have an undeniably Romantic point of view. It is evident in the voluptuous texture and tenderness, the complexity, and the yearning for the past that is shown in their works. Yet, in sculpture, more than in any other art form, it is clearly impossible

to place the various 19th-century tendencies int
neat pigeonholes.

A group of French sculptors set themselves u
as the standard-bearers of the Romantic cause
In opposition to the ancient ideal of beauty, the
favored the following traits: the freedom to us
concrete contemporary themes; a preference fo

CHRISTIAN RAUCH and others. *Monument to Frederick the Great.* **1839-52. East Berlin.**
Rauch is one of many sculptors unquestionably categorized as Classical. This monument is a typical example of 19th-century commemorative sculpture. This is not an isolated statue, merely dressed in the clothes of another time. Rather, it is a more complex work of art, full of symbolism and detail, and it must be appreciated in relationship to its site.

tension and movement; a curiosity about th
imperfect, even the grotesque; a renunciation o
strict rules of anatomy and composition; a searc
for pictorial and expressive effects; and the rep
resentation of all types of emotion. These sculp
tors were interested in new forms of expression
Although some of the sculptors were initiall
rejected, all of them were eventually accepted int
the artistic community and, in fact, their idea
finally triumphed. Even though these new idea
were systematically adopted by all sculptors
there was not much substantial change in sculp
tural imagery. Whatever their original trainin
and intentions, these sculptors are usually calle
Eclectic and theirs was a period of borrowing an
of blending.

ANTOINE-LOUIS BARYE. *Angelica and Roger.* **1840. The Louvre, Paris.**

This is an illustration of a scene from *Orlando Furioso*, a novel by the Italian writer Ludovico Ariosto. Roger, one of the characters, has just freed Angelica, who had been chained naked on an island. They are fleeing with the help of a dolphin that also serves as a base. This use of a theme from a novel is typical of Romantic inspiration, but the most notable element here is the power of Barye's animals, even mythological ones. He made detailed studies of animals, copied them carefully, and transmitted in his bronze sculptures the impetuousness and violence of nature, thus fusing the Romantic spirit with Naturalist detail.

HONORÉ DAUMIER.
Ratapoil. c. 1850. Musée
d'Orsay, Paris.
Daumier was not interested
in the technical problems
that obsessed other sculptors of his period. Because
of that, his work seems to
be the most avant-garde of
the century. He appears to
have had a deep knowledge
of, or at least a great insight
into, the possibilities of
sculpture, and he aban-
doned any attempt at
representational art. The
feeling of caricature in this
piece—which is so similar
to his drawings and paintings—gives a freshness to
a matchless work of art.

In most countries there was little inclination to
distinguish between the Romantic spirit found
in **Classicism** and that found in Electicism. The
term *Eclectic* best defines most 19th-century
sculpture stylistically, because models from the
past were repeated, and many stylistic stereotypes
were used simultaneously. During this period, the
formal values inherent in sculpture—such as the
texture of the material—were often ignored in the
search for scenic, narrative effects. Simplicity was
avoided in favor of showing off all kinds of technical skills. The composition of 19th-century
works is usually complex and full of movement,
and the pieces often arouse strong emotions in
the spectator—sometimes even erotic ones.

Realist sculptors were more interested in theme
or subject than in formal innovation. Even if their
themes were different, they are still basically considered Eclectic artists. The desire for truth in art—
which was identified as dressing characters in
modern clothes or portraying some aspect of
daily life—had existed in France from the 1830s.
This interest in genre—rustic visions of shep-
herds, fishers, or people in the trades—gradually
widened to include the "objective" representation
of all social classes, from the middle class to the
manual laborers. Special mention must be made
of the role of the Belgian sculptor Constantin
Meunier. His representation of workers in industrial society is not picturesque. Honest toil had
become a symbol of a new force.

Sculpture from the second half of the 19th century exhibits values that deserve mention. Without them, the regeneration in sculpture that
happened at the turn of the century cannot be
understood. One of these values was the break-
down of any distinction between worthy and

unworthy subjects. All themes became acceptable. This spirit of a new reality, as seen in the work
of Honoré Daumier and Jean-Baptiste Carpeaux,
continued in the work of late 19th-century sculptors such as Medardo Rosso and Auguste Rodin.

Besides analyzing styles and subjects, we need
to consider the functional diversity of 19th-
century sculpture. As in all art of the century—
particularly in architecture, but in painting as
well—there exists a link between form and function. Above all else, a 19th-century sculpture
was required to function as an object of beauty,
which means sculpture had become essentially
decorative.

**CONSTANTIN
MEUNIER. *Dock Worker
from the Port of Antwerp.*
1885. Musée National de
l'Art Moderne, Paris.**
Meunier's figures show the
effects of Realism on sculpture. In their solitary splendor, they appear ennobled
by work, yet not pompous.
It is interesting to note that
by omitting such things as
attention to minute detail
and a pedestal, Meunier
was taking the first steps
toward a new appreciation
of volume in a new space.

JEAN-BAPTISTE CARPEAUX. *The Dance.* **1869. Paris.**
This work was commissioned for the new Opera, which was designed by Charles Garnier. Its sensuality of movement is reminiscent of Peter-Paul Rubens, and this, coupled with the ambiguity of the central figure and the lecherous smiles of the women, suggests an orgy. The work provoked strong puritanical criticism when it first appeared.

There are two facets to this decorative aspect of 19th-century sculpture. One can be found in the technical, creative process and the traditional relationship between the artist and his or her method of working. For sculptors, this involved personal contact with their work—from a beginning sketch to carving the finished piece or creating the model from which stone or cast bronze pieces were made.

The second part of the decorative aspect is found in the essential intimacy of much 19th century sculpture. This played a vital part in the development of portrait busts and statuettes. They conveyed various themes, which suited the taste of the middle class. The portrait bust was the most appropriate artistic subject for the Romantics. Portrait busts seemed more permanent than paintings. In busts, the careful arrangement of elements was the most important aspect: the most flattering physical features, the hair style, the dress, and, above all, the gesture depicted. Indeed, one of the annual competitions held by the School of Beaux Arts required artists to demonstrate their ability to depict various emotions in busts—pain or violence, for example.

An overview of 19th-century sculpture would be incomplete without a study of the great political and religious architectural commissions given to sculptors. Public sculptures on urban monuments and in cemeteries have left a record that demonstrates the close link between sculpture and architecture of the 19th century. We need to understand the sculptural **iconography** in relationship to buildings and monuments in order to appreciate the two arts as a whole.

RICARDO BELLVER. *The Fallen Angel.* 1876. Madrid.
The artist won first prize with this work in the 1876 National Exhibition, and it is one of the greatest examples of 19th-century Spanish art. Bellver used a nude (depicted with clear anatomical detail) in a contorted position to portray a provocative theme. The pedestal, too, forms an important part of the whole work. Designed by the architect Francisco Jareño, it is an integral part of the sculpture, not merely a support for the figure. The whole is the result of collaboration between architect and sculptor. They decreed that the statue should stand by itself and gave precise measurements and details of what was required for its placement.

The urban monument best typifies 19th-century art: it is widespread, varied in its development, and carries many artistic and nonartistic implications. Monuments that were commissioned or were erected as part of competitions represent the values of the city dweller. They are indispensable if a city is to distinguish itself from other cities. They remind citizens of the glories of the past and of the virtues of their ancestors. In many ways, the cemetery is an idealized 19th-century city. The cemetery was often organized along the same lines as a city and was a place

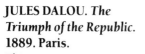

JULES DALOU. *The Triumph of the Republic.* 1889. Paris.
This monument represents the chariot of the Republic, guided by the spirit of Liberty, accompanied by figures representing Work, Justice, and Peace (or Plenty). The work was paid for by the city of Paris after a competition—even though Dalou had lost the competition for such a monument. The courtly Baroque style harks back to the times of Louis XIV in its attempt to capture the imagination of the masses.

where architecture could express itself in the wildest extremes of Eclecticism. The multitude of frozen, almost magical figures hidden away in niches and tombs gives cemeteries their sentimental and moral dimensions. There are representations of the dear departed—sometimes merely solemn and often heartbreakingly realistic. The mythical figures, such as angels and funeral symbols, seem to fuse architecture and vegetation together into a vague frontier between vanity and deification.

PAINTING

Throughout the 19th century, painters concerned themselves with two questions: Should artists make use of all knowledge acquired since the Renaissance and adapt it to their own time? Or, should they free painting from the traditional restraints and search for a new definition of basic concepts?

Debates on these questions took place throughout the Western world, though in different forms. Art had become international, and although Paris was often considered to be at the center of the debate, it wasn't necessarily true that whatever was happening in Paris was also happening elsewhere. Nevertheless, Paris became the reference point for new ideas.

Romantics or Eclectics?

Romantic elements can be found in many paintings since the turn of the century. Although Théodore Géricault's *Raft of the Medusa* (1819) is considered to be the first great expression of Romanticism in painting, earlier works could well be classified as Romantic. The works of John Henry Fuseli or William Blake, for example, contain Romantic elements, such as dreamlike, angry images of the naked ego and also sublime visions of the universe.

The greatest extremes of the Romantic vision of nature—and people's attitude toward it—can be seen in the landscapes of the German artist

JOHN CONSTABLE.
Dedham Vale. **1828.**
National Gallery of
Scotland, Edinburgh.
Constable avoided stereotypes and depicted an emotional appreciation of nature, as did all Romantics. He planned his compositions carefully—the horizon, trees, the placement of buildings, rivers, and animals—but still conveyed a deep, contemplative sensitivity to nature. His work presents an accumulation of visual experiences in which color takes on tonal values that are, in turn, almost independent of what is being depicted.

Caspar David Friedrich. The surroundings in his works are distant, wide, immense, almost infinite. The human being, within the composition or without, contemplates the sublime silence of the countryside, the deep melancholy of natural phenomena, the mist over the mountains, the splendor of a sunset, or the virgin snow in a winter landscape. No one uses the forces of nature better than Friedrich to express the anxieties and incomprehension of the individual.

Filled with some of these same anxieties, a group of German artists banded together on July 10, 1809, in Vienna. The next year they moved to Rome and set themselves up in the Monastery of San Isidoro. This group became known as the Nazarenes. Their objective was to move toward a sincere restoration of Christian art through the use of medieval forms. They admired German and Italian paintings of the Middle Ages and the early Renaissance.

Their results, later converted into a teaching system closely linked to academic tendencies,

THÉODORE GÉRICAULT. *The Raft of the Medusa.* **1819. The Louvre, Paris.**

In this very significant work, Géricault is influenced by some Neoclassic techniques, but the spirit and effect of the painting are radically different. The diagonal composition and the treatment of the human forms use pictorial elements in a new and purposeful way. Géricault chose as his subject a recent shipwreck, a contemporary event. The survivors, seeing a possible rescue ship, try to attract its attention, but, unsure about being seen, they are plunged into despair. This is a Romantic painting, filled with human crises.

EUGÈNE DELACROIX. *The Death of Sardanapolus.* **1828. The Louvre, Paris.**

Few works combine so many and such deeply expressed characteristics of Romantic painting. Here, form is extremely dynamic, bordering on complete disorder. The figures move with dramatic tension, and the brushstrokes of rich color are applied freely. The theme shares this feverish movement: the dying ruler, contemplating his forthcoming death, orders an orgy. The whole atmosphere is charged with sensuality and violence—heightened by the contrast between the virility of the slaves and the voluptuousness of the harem women.

**JEAN-AUGUSTE-
DOMINIQUE INGRES.**
The Turkish Bath.
**1859-63. The Louvre,
Paris.**
The Source. **1820-56.
Musée d'Orsay. Paris.**
Until his death in 1867,
Ingres was the embodiment
of most of the ideals of
Neoclassicism. An idealized
view of nature and drawing
as the basis for all art are
two of Ingres's main characteristics. His themes,
however, are no different
from those made fashiona-
ble by the Romantics, and

promoted a method using religious narrative
and a relatively primitive approach. Art histori
ans now regard the Nazarenes as stereotyped
affected, and pretentious—the very qualities the
were trying to fight against.

From the beginning of the 19th century, paint
ing showed an increasing awareness of nature
Nature was endowed with the attributes of poetr
and was skillfully portrayed—two characteristic
which are important when categorizing Roman
ticism in paintings. Sometimes artists tried to cap
ture the mystical poetry of the countryside and
its inhabitants by presenting every detail, so min
ute and complete that the results tended to go
beyond a mere appreciation of the scene.

John Constable and Joseph Mallord Willian
Turner are important English landscape artists
They were the inheritors of a long British tradi
tion of fluid, light painting and a pleasurable and
respectful admiration for the countryside, trees
animals, water, sky, and clouds. Never before had

in this and other ways, he is a product of his age. His Romanticism is not limited to subject matter, however. Although the discovery of the natural appeal of the nude body came from academic teaching, Ingres imbued these forms with a sensual line and soft surface. Middle-class society was prepared to tolerate—even to enjoy—these voluptuous, relaxed, carefree women, because they were placed in an exotic Oriental setting.

painting achieved such complete harmony of color and composition with purely visual effects. The role of Constable and Turner is indispensible in understanding the changes that have taken place in modern art.

PAUL DELAROCHE.
Execution of Lady Jane Grey. **1834. The National Gallery, London.**
From the point of view of the public and officialdom, the most important kind of Romantic art was historical painting. It was common practice to look for paral-

lels between the events of the present and those of the past. During the first decades of the 19th century, the history of England was a popular subject among French painters. Delaroche repeatedly used British themes and combined academic practice with the

characteristics of Naturalism. He was very skillful at capturing emotions, and he realized an exquisite precision in his exact, detailed depictions of individual objects. He had many imitators in all countries.

In France, by the 1820s, a tendency had begun to characterize paintings as Romantic either by their compositions or their subjects. For example, in the works of Pierre-Paul Prud'hon héodore Géricault, and above all, Eugène Delacroix, it was possible to recognize a new chool by its use of color, turbulent compositions, brilliant brushstrokes spreading beyond the dges of the forms, and themes with exceptionlly picturesque or literary character. Delacroix mmediately became the standard-bearer of this novement, which opposed those who maintained he Neoclassical ideals of design. A controversy petween these two attitudes was encouraged by ritics who claimed to recognize a Romantic style.

ut we should not read too much into this controversy. Although Romantic influences increased hroughout the 19th century, we should be on ur guard about viewing the ideals of that century from our own perspective.

French painters tried to combine distinctive lements from both tendencies. Thomas Couture, n ambitious and talented painter, exercised a nique role in this. He combined lessons from ast masters with bold, insistent brushstrokes. lis teachings spread around the world and influnced a new type of painting—one based on acalemic principles, but having its own original parkle. This style became very popular during he second half of the 19th century.

THOMAS COUTURE.
The Romans of the Decadence. **1847.**
Musée d'Orsay, Paris.
This painting was one of the most famous works of art of the 19th century. Contemporaries especially valued what constituted a system of painting that could be taught and learned—a system based on famous past masters whose influence could be readily seen and understood. The ability to imitate previous great works and to combine them with a theme— both erotic and moral— appealed to the imagination of a society that reveled in exaggerated and spectacular subjects. Couture was an ambitious painter with great virtuosity, a shaper of Eclecticism, and an important teacher.

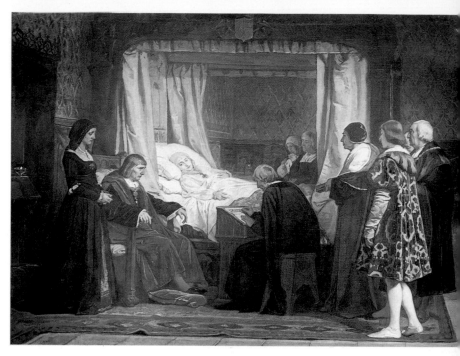

EDUARDO ROSALES.
The Testament of Isabel the Catholic. **1864.**
Casón, Madrid.
Rosales played an essential role in 19th-century Spanish painting and its attempts to absorb foreign styles (especially those of France) and to produce a new interpretation of national traditions. In this work, both the formal and ideological aspects of historical painting are present. Note the emphasis on space as a cube, the attention to detail of objects, and the attitudes of the figures. Rosales's portrayal offers an obvious lesson for modern society: respect for a queen, who, even at the moment of her death, is still concerned about the destiny of the nation and shows a deep love for her people.

From Realism to Impressionism

The urge to create a vision of nature that was unhampered either by academic convention or Romantic effects grew strong in the middle of the 19th century. The origin of this Realistic representation of nature is to be found in the Barbizon school. There are as many Romantic and Classical elements in the works of the Barbizon artists as there are Naturalistic

CHARLES FRANÇOIS DAUBIGNY. *Landscape with a Rainbow.* **1860. Art Institute, Chicago.**
Daubigny holds a very special place in the development of French outdoor painting. He is a direct inheritor of the experiences of the Barbizon school in depicting the natural environment without following set rules. Daubigny was especially interested in an analysis of light on objects and on the atmosphere—an interest he also managed to translate through the technique of drawing.

ones. There are also references to traditional landscapes—particularly those from 17th-century Holland and those by Nicolas Poussin and Claude Lorrain. Even though there is a romanticizing of natural elements—luxuriant trees, roads, mountains, rivers, and clouds—in contrast to previous painters, Realist artists were constantly exploring ways of transferring to canvas all the varied facets of nature. Camille Corot made a great contribution to this fusion of styles by incorporating the ideals of Classicism into the direct observation of what he saw, expressed in terms of color and light.

CAMILLE COROT. *The Shepherd's Star.* **1864. Museum of Toulouse, Toulouse.**
Corot made a very personal and exceptional contribution to the process of realistically depicting what an artist sees. Several, sometimes contradictory, elements are involved in his work, including a balance between the unchanging and the transient, the appearance of objects in relation to the light, and the replacement of drawing with the application of large masses of color. The vitality of his paintings and their subjects goes far beyond any idealism. All his work has an air of simplicity and serenity.

FRANZ XAVIER WINTERHALTER. *The Empress Eugenie with Her Ladies in Waiting.* **c. 1860. Chateau of Compiègne, Compiègne.**

During the latter years of the 19th century, Winterhalter was the most sought-after portrait painter among the aristocracy of Europe. His portraits have all the characteristics of Romanticism: a faithful representation of physical reality, with a tendency toward idealization; an emphasis on mood; and the use of light to create a circle that the spectator cannot penetrate. He

placed his subjects in somewhat intimate poses and used technical perfection and scenic effects in a seemingly casual way. His portraits are usually superficially brilliant, but they lack creativity.

JEAN-FRANÇOIS MILLET. *The Angelus.* **1858-59. The Louvre, Paris.**

The significance of Millet's work remains ambiguous—something that happens with any artist whom we try to identify exclusively with one style. Although Millet was in contact with the Barbizon group, he was essentially a painter of ideas. Like most Romantics, he tried to express ideas through form. He did not think of nature as something that can be represented. His basic theme was peasants, whom he portrayed working or involved in some everyday

activity. His use of special light, the blurring of contours, and a low horizon all alter reality, almost to the point of giving it a religious dignity and glorification. The life in Millet's canvas is real, and its subject (in spite of similarities to works of earlier painters) is revolutionary. His work always appears idyllic—the ideal 19th-century rustic paradise.

48

Although it is in paintings of the countryside hat this move toward reality is most easily seen, ther themes were equally important for the Realsts. Jean-François Millet, who also was a member of the Barbizon group, painted peasants. le did the most to popularize a relatively new neme—one that moved away from the Romantic enre paintings of customs and manners, but can e definitely classified as Realist.

Another painter whose work illustrates the cope and variety of 19th-century styles is Honoré aumier. Born in 1808, he was a contemporary f many Romantic painters. The themes he chose

HONORÉ DAUMIER.
Rue Transnonain,
15th April, 1834.
Death is a recurring theme in art. The Romantics managed to transform it by justifying it in terms of love or ideals. In Realism, it appears as a trivial incident. This lithograph by Daumier was inspired by an event that happened in the reign of Louis Phillipe. During an uprising in a working-class area of Paris, a soldier was shot. In retaliation, his comrades killed all the occupants of a house. In this image of the anti-hero, of brutality and injustice, Daumier demonstrates the revolutionary possibilities of art from a political viewpoint.

he daily life of ordinary people, people in the reets, at work, or on trains) make him appear be a Realist. His drawings (often caricatures) id the crude satire of some of his figures attack le very basis of society. On the other hand, the notion in his allegorical and religious works akes Daumier an artist difficult to classify. mong his contemporaries, few artists aroused ich great interest.

Gustave Courbet's paintings are firmly Realist; fact, his name became synonymous with Realm. His works best show the characteristics of at movement, although his art is obviously

MARIANO FORTUNY.
The Spanish Wedding.
1870. Museum of Modern Art, Barcelona.

One current of 19th-century Spanish art that had great success in Europe was a form of Realism known as "cabinet painting." Its founder was Fortuny, whose paintings are small and generally depict 18th-century costumed scenes. In them, minor events are treated with great care and are extremely detailed. The paintings link elements of Romantic poetry with Realist innovations—broad brushstrokes and casual placement of figures within the composition.

GUSTAVE COURBET.
Burial in Ornans. **1850.**
Musée d'Orsay, Paris.
This work shows a
common event—a village
funeral. There are no recognizable people, the figures
are not arranged in any
order of importance, and
the twilight is used solely
to outline the physical
forms of the participants
and to convey the solitude
of the countryside. There is
no great drama, and the
people have no symbolic
meaning—they are depicted
as they are.

GIOVANNI FATTORI. *La Rotonda Palmieri.* **1866. Gallery of Modern Art, Florence.**

Fattori is the most important artist in a group of Italian painters called the Macchiaioli. They brought together aspects of the new open-air style, like this scene on a beach. They used the most brilliant colors, ignored tone and line in favor of blurred outlines, and produced paintings based on broad areas of color altered by light. The commonplace nature of their themes did not diminish the feeling of richness and freedom from restraint in their work. In this canvas our experience is almost exclusively one of color and light.

influenced by past "Realist" schools, notably the Dutch and the Spanish. Courbet was a splendid revolutionary in technique, form, and iconography. This is seen in his appreciation of thick layers of paint, in the casual composition of his pictures, and in the absence of "acceptable" subjects. The content and themes of his work reject both the accepted portrayal of beauty and the presence of an ideal world. This rejection was depicted by direct representations of whatever affected modern life: work and the worker portrayed as the new, "ordinary" hero; outdoor life (beaches, picnics); town life (street scenes, cafes, dances); the family; and the woman of the world. He even depicted death as the trivial end of life as opposed to an end that had been considered glorious.

WILHELM LEIBL. *Three Women in Church.* **1878-82. Kunsthalle, Hamburg.**

Leibl was a follower of Courbet, particularly in his use of color and theme. However, unlike the French artist, the German painter Leibl executed each element in this oil painting with photographic precision and with a Naturalist's eye. He was obsessed with microscopic details and used them to raise a simple theme to a sublime level.

ÉDOUARD MANET.
Le Déjeuner sur l'Herbe.
**1863. Musée du Jeu
de Paume, Paris.**
Manet was exceptional in
synthesizing the pictorial
ideas of past masters,
including those of his
teacher, Thomas Couture.
But Manet almost com-
pletely abandoned the tonal
gradation of color—a fun-
damental of academic
teaching since the begin-
ning of the century. Instead,
he favored the construction
of a picture based on flat
planes, whose importance
he began to realize intui-
tively. If any artist sums up
the division between the
past and the present in
19th-century art, it is

Courbet's painting represented the first sudden break in the accepted concept of a work o
art. But Western painting did not follow Courbet
guidelines exclusively, because Realist experi
ments were taking place all over Europe durin
the second half of the 19th century. In these exper
iments, a relationship between light and colo
appears to have developed independently o
Courbet's strong influence. The **Pre-Raphaelite**
in England can be considered Realists because o
their declaration of sincerity, their faithfulness t
nature (instead of following academic rules), an
their treatment of themes. Yet their ideas an
works are the opposite of Courbet's, because the
have a more intellectual, escapist, and symboli
preoccupation.

The two most important consequences of Real
ism were: first, a change in acceptable subjec
matter—any subject was now valid, and therefor
the importance of subject matter decreased; an

econd, the dissolution of what until then had een stereotyped representations of reality. No uropean painter or critic could fail to be influnced by these revolutionary aspects in painting ven if only to be on guard against them.

Another result of the introduction of Courbet's ealism was that more and more individual styles eveloped, making it difficult to identify the most authentic" Realist artists. For example, German Jaturalism brought together all the clichés of he Realist spirit in its insistence on the imporance of the medium and casual composition. An nteresting group of painters, called the Italian

art, it is Manet; his fantastic accomplishment was in synthesizing them—in bringing the elements of the past and the present together.

CLAUDE MONET. *Rouen Cathedral: Morning Effect.* **1892-94. Musée d'Orsay, Paris.**
In this painting, light and color create a certain atmosphere. The Gothic form of the cathedral at Rouen offered Monet a perfect model for study. In less than two years he painted 20 versions of this cathedral. He was not interested in the building itself, but in the variations of atmosphere created by the changing play of color and light on the building at different times of day.

PIERRE-AUGUSTE RENOIR. *Moulin de la Galette.* **1876. Musée d'Orsay, Paris.**
The Moulin, a small, modest dance hall in Paris, was visited by workers, students, and artists living nearby. This canvas portrays customers sitting at their tables or dancing. The sunlight falling through the leaves casts dappled shadows in various tones. Critics at the time spoke of "figures dancing on a surface resembling the violet clouds which cover the sky just before a thunderstorm."

ognizable features or from symbolic messages. This painting represents the forces of nature and the new feelings of modern people, who could travel at previously unheard-of speeds. In Turner's later works, the subject and the form became almost one in an Expressionist manner. His art has been described as the vision of a dream changed into a painting a moment before awakening.

JOSEPH MALLORD WILLIAM TURNER. *Storm at Sea.* **1840. Tate Gallery, London.**
Turner never completely managed to divorce his paintings from visible, rec-

Macchiaioli, reduced their painted surfaces t brilliant contrasts of solid areas of color. The stressed the objective representation of the pla of light on objects. This preoccupation with ligh shared by many Realists, was adopted as funda mental by the French Impressionists.

The Impressionist painters, among whom wer Claude Monet, Pierre-Auguste Renoir, Camill Pissarro, Edgar Degas, and the Englishman Alfre

Sisley, exhibited together between 1874 and 1886.
Each then went his own way. (Manet was a friend
of these artists and was influenced by them, but
he never exhibited with them.) Their aim was to
capture the immediate impression of a scene.
They often worked outdoors and used a rapid
and direct technique of easy flowing brushstrokes
and pure colors. In general, an Impressionist work
could be described as being preoccupied more

EDGAR DEGAS. *The Glass of Absinthe.* 1876. The Louvre, Paris.
Two Blue Ballerinas. Van der Hegolt Museum, Wuppertal.

It is said that on one occasion, a lady aggressively asked Degas why the women he painted were so ugly. "Madame," he replied, "because women usually are ugly." Whether true or not, this story illustrates one essential facet of the French avant-garde artists: the beauty of a painting is in the painting itself and not in what it represents. This attitude reveals a strong emphasis upon the formal qualities of a work as opposed to the subject matter. Degas is an exception within the Impressionist group. He preferred the human form to landscape, artificial light to natural light, drawing to patches of color, and strange and fragmentary poses to the everyday pose—particularly if the latter carried any literary message. What he shared with the Impressionists were his palette and his technique of applying the pigment to the canvas. His images are sometimes critical and direct.

with the value of light and atmosphere than with subject. Impressionism must be understood within the context of its time. It is tied to the history, politics, and crises of the Second Empire in France and to philosophical questions about time and space. Impressionism was also influenced by scientific and technological developments, such as new theories on color, paint in tubes, and the explosion of a new art form—photography.

Landscapes were the Impressionists' favorite theme. Everyday subjects and events were chosen, and all were depicted according to the time of day, the natural light, and the mist or clouds present. Stylistically, the Impressionists preferred soft brushstrokes and color and light over tight

ANTONIO MUÑOZ DEGRAIN. *Gleaners from Jericho.* **Museo de Bellas Artes, Valencia.**
The appreciation of natural and luminous qualities in painting was a general preoccupation of late 19th-century artists, though it often took seemingly diverging roads. In a mixture of Realist and Impressionist styles, Muñoz Degrain used colors that transcend those of nature in brilliance and have an almost magical property.

draftsmanship. They sought out reflected light and its effect on color, and they abhorred black. Impressionism is the last tenuous link between painting and the visible world as it was understood at the time; and with an almost exclusive emphasis on form, color and light, it began the destruction of that world for painters.

Symbolists and Idealists

During the second half of the 19th century, another artistic style developed—**Symbolism.** It was an intellectual movement, thoroughly escapist, and interested in aesthetics and—as its name states—symbols. It was a direct descendant of Romanticism and showed a tendency to move away from the formalism of the academy.

In 1848, seven artists joined together in London to form the Pre-Raphaelite Brotherhood. The core of the group consisted of Dante Gabriel Rossetti, William Holman Hunt, and John Everett Millais. Their aim was to bring a new moral seriousness

PIERRE PUVIS DE CHAVANNES. *Childhood of Saint Genevieve.* **1877. Pantheon, Paris.**
The most famous works of Puvis de Chavannes are his canvas murals which he executed for various public buildings. The Third Republic undertook the task of decorating the old Pantheon with paintings in which French nationalism and religion would be linked. Many well-known painters took part in the project, which shows how Symbolism could adapt to officialdom. It distanced itself from traditional, official imagery, however, by renouncing scenic effects in favor of primitivism, simplicity, and serenity.

ɔ painting. The members studied directly from ature and cast aside stereotyped academic rules. or five years, they sought inspiration in the vorks of Italian painters of the Middle Ages nd the early Renaissance, as had the German Nazarenes. They worked with bright, clear colrs, which gained luminosity by being applied to white ground. Their religious and literary hemes were treated in a Naturalist style. The rotherhood ended in 1862 with the death of ,izzie Siddal, Rossetti's wife, who had been a najor inspiration for the group.

DANTE GABRIEL ROSSETTI. *Beata Beatrix.* **c. 1863. Tate Gallery, London.**
The curious beauty of Lizzie Siddal haunted the Pre-Raphaelites. Rossetti met her in 1850, and she posed for many works by him as well as Holman Hunt and John Everett Millais. She married Rossetti in 1860 and died two years later from a drug overdose. *Beata Beatrix,* painted after her death, is perhaps the last of Rossetti's inspired works. Heavily charged with symbolism, it reveals the ideal of womanhood that dominated the Pre-Raphaelite group—an idol, unaffected by emotion, adored solely for her irresistible presence. Rossetti depicted his wife at the moment of her death—in an ecstatic state with her head thrown back and lips parted. The haloed bird is the messenger of death, and it drops a white poppy into her hands, a symbol of passion and an allusion to the opium that killed her.

On the continent, some German painters maintained the Germanic tradition of regarding Rome and academic styles with reverence, while other exhibited a more pompous Eclecticism. Symbolism was not a major concern for them. However in France, Symbolism found important followers who were opposed to Realism, although their work coincided with the later stages of Realism development. As in other countries, Realism appeared to be more closely linked to official circles, salons, and commissions.

Gustave Moreau was one of the key figures of the French Symbolist movement. Moreau's point of departure was Romantic. He was attracted by the fervent, colorful world of Eugène Delacroix and the sensual orientalism of Théodore Chasseriau. Although Moreau's work has a literary air (it is full of hints about beauty and love, life and death), his contribution to the pictorial field was very important. Moreau's canvasses combine sensuousness with intellectual provocation. The refined richness of his colors and the languid grace of his heroes create a curious world of their own.

Clearly distinct from the precious surfaces of Moreau are the rigidly classical compositions of Pierre Puvis de Chavannes. The most important quality of his works was the balanced structure of painted areas. His paintings, often excessively artificial because of their conventional symbolism, reside in an absolute vacuum. There is no movement, no light, no volume; and the colors are flat and lusterless. One gets the impression from his work that painting had broken with representational art, and modern painting had already been born.

DRAWINGS AND SKETCHES

**ODILON REDON:
Cactus Man. Woodner
Collection.**

Redon was one of the
strangest of the Symbolists.
Their inclination toward
the world of dreams and
the unreal became so
disquieting that the
ultimate meaning of their
work became almost
indecipherable. When
Redon's art seeks to translate a literary work into a
visual work, it is unfathom-
ble. This impenetrability,
however, has its own power
and attraction and, at times,
even a touch of lyricism.

**HENRI FANTIN-
LATOUR. *Portrait of
Madame Ditte*. Woodner
Collection.**

Fantin-Latour is a singular
figure in French painting.
He is proof that, besides the
Impressionists, there were
other interesting, restless
painters experimenting
along different lines.
Although a companion of
the Impressionists, he often
used a deliberately photographic technique in his
work—an echo of lingering
traditions.

There are three important reasons for studying 19th-century drawings and sketches.
First, drawing was considered an important academic subject, both in its own right and
as a preparatory stage for a finished painting. All
students of art studied drawing as part of their
training to understand perspective, composition,
volume and space, and how these elements had
been treated by the old masters. Second, paral-
leling what we have seen in painting, we can trace
the revolution that took place and released drawing from the constrictions of conventions. The
value of nonlinear principles was recognized.

FERDINAND KHNOPFF.
Who Shall Deliver Me?
**1891. N. Manukian
Collection, Paris.**
All Symbolist works show
an almost uncontrollable
yearning for a world
beyond human experience,
a desire to express that
which lies beyond the
senses. The very term,
Symbolist, refers to something that goes beyond
physical reality. This is
depicted in painting by a
wealth of magical worlds
such as artificial landscapes
and voluptuous, exotic,
or dreamlike decorations.
The involvement with the
extrasensory world also
led to an interest in religion
and mythology, and images
of those realms are often
found in the works of
Khnopff.

Third, even though drawings and sketches have
always been of great interest to art historians (for
one thing, they show the first ideas that underlie
finished works), their value increased during the
19th century. Instead of being considered mere
preparatory studies, the brilliance and originality of sketches gave them greater importance.
Sketches became works of art in their own right.

THE ART OF
REPRODUCING IMAGES

A great revolution in 19th-century art was caused by new developments in the process of printing and the subsequent ability to create multiple, identical images. Interesting in their own right, these achievements had an impact that makes them fundamentally important to the history of art as a whole.

CARLOS LUIS DE RIBERA. Cover for the magazine *El Artista*. 1834.
Illustrated magazines began to become important with the growth of the Romantic movement. *El Artista* was one of the first to print and distribute the new artistic ideas. The magazine was moderately liberal and clearly leaned toward artistic Eclecticism, which was common to the whole Romantic movement in Spain. Other periodicals that appeared during the century catered to middle-class tastes and spread and popularized a knowledge of the past and of art.

Woodcuts, which had been made since the end of the 13th century, came back into fashion during the first half of the 19th century. But it was wood engraving that became popular. The technology of papermaking was also refined. The thickness and texture of paper, for example, became more uniform. This improved the quality of the final image and facilitated the reproduction process.

In metalworking, changes also took place with the rediscovery of the art of engraving and etching. New printing presses were made of steel, and waterproof inks were developed. Above all, steel engravings made mass production of well-illustrated books a possibility.

The art of caricature formed an essential part of the critical self-consciousness of the 19th century, and its effectiveness was entirely dependent on being able to be reproduced and distributed in great numbers. In France, Honoré Daumier stands out among the caricaturists who ridiculed many aspects of the daily life of his society.

In 1796, the technique of lithography was invented, and its development had far-reaching effects. Lithography allowed artists to reproduce details of any event very rapidly. As a reproductive technique, it was easier than either wood or metal printing, and it soon became extremely valuable as a means of illustrating books.

None of the new methods of reproduction, however, could compare with photography. Although the first experimental photographs concentrated on lifeless landscapes and town views, the most frequent early use of the camera was for portraiture. Painters increasingly influenced portrait photography, especially as far as poses and backgrounds were concerned.

By far the greatest interest in photography focused on its effect on the traditional ways of representing the visible world. The invention of photography and a taste for minute descriptions of detail went hand in hand in many art forms—literature, painting, and sculpture. Many Realist painters even used photographs as an aid to capturing the appearance of their world, and this use contributed to the acceptance of the new medium. Technical improvements contributed not only to the popularity of photography, but also to the establishment of photography as an art.

Photography and painting developed a close relationship. Early photographers were strongly influenced by contemporary paintings. In a similar way, the direct and decisive nature of photography—its ability to capture detailed images—

**GUSTAVE DORÉ.
Illustration for Milton's
Paradise Lost. 1866.**
Gustave Doré, although a painter, too, was best known for his illustrations of major literary works. His training as an illustrator minimized the effect of avant-garde art on his work, which reflected already well-established stereotypes. He was extraordinarily prolific, and his work became known throughout the world. Given the nature of his work—printed illustrations—his huge output was completed with the efforts of many collaborating artists. In his images, he often reaches heights of fantastic exuberance, and reality begins to merge with dreams.

influenced painters. As the ability of photographs to capture the visible world increased, painters felt less necessity to imitate it, and they began to wrestle with other artistic questions. Simultaneously, photography showed that our vision of reality is made up not of line but of light—objects and colors are a function of light.

The ability to print from photographs also had

WILLIAM MORRIS. Illustrated page from Kelmscott Press. Kelmscott Manor was a luxurious medieval-style mansion acquired by Morris in 1871 in partnership with the Pre-Raphaelite Rossetti. The name *Kelmscott* was given to the press, which published, among other items, love stories. The publication was carefully designed and included perfectly executed illustrations and covers. Though influenced by many older ideas, these publications shared the new interest in the art of the book and combined text and image into exquisite creations.

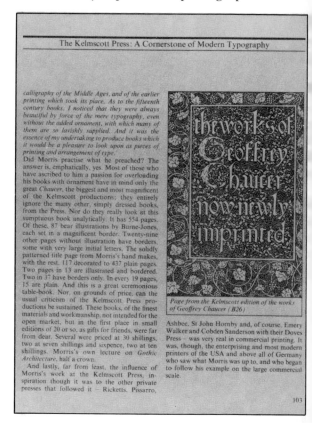

The Kelmscott Press: A Cornerstone of Modern Typography

calligraphy of the Middle Ages, and of the earlier printing which took its place. As to the fifteenth century books, I noticed that they were always beautiful by force of the mere typography, even without the added ornament, with which many of them are so lavishly supplied. And it was the essence of my undertaking to produce books which it would be a pleasure to look upon as pieces of printing and arrangement of type.

Did Morris practise what he preached? The answer is, emphatically, yes. Most of those who have ascribed to him a passion for overloading his books with ornament have in mind only the great *Chaucer*, the biggest and most magnificent of the Kelmscott productions; they entirely ignore the many other, simply dressed books, from the Press. Nor do they really look at this sumptuous book analytically. It has 554 pages. Of these, 87 bear illustrations by Burne-Jones, each set in a magnificent border. Twenty-nine other pages without illustration have borders, some with very large initial letters. The solidly patterned title page from Morris's hand makes, with the rest, 117 decorated to 437 plain pages. Two pages in 13 are illustrated and bordered. Two in 37 have borders only. In every 19 pages, 15 are plain. And this is a great ceremonious table-book. Nor, on grounds of price, can the usual criticism of the Kelmscott Press productions be sustained. These books, of the finest materials and workmanship, not intended for the open market, but in the first place in small editions of 20 or so, as gifts for friends, were far from dear. Several were priced at 30 shillings, two at seven shillings and sixpence, two at ten shillings. Morris's own lecture on *Gothic Architecture*, half a crown.

And lastly, far from least, the influence of Morris's work at the Kelmscott Press, inspiration though it was to the other private presses that followed it — Ricketts, Pissarro,

Page from the Kelmscott edition of the works of Geoffrey Chaucer (B26)

Ashbee, St John Hornby and, of course, Emery Walker and Cobden Sanderson with their Doves Press — was very real in commercial printing. It was, though, the enterprising and most modern printers of the USA and above all of Germany who saw what Morris was up to, and who began to follow his example on the large commercial scale.

103

a great effect. Experiments in the last years of the 19th century with phototypography and photolithography made possible the reproduction of any natural or artistic object. That meant that for the first time, an identical image could reach thousands of people. A totally new and unexpected element in our culture had been born.

DECORATIVE ART

The decorative arts flourished and prolif-
erated during the 19th century. However,
the whole debate on the role of art during
that period also affected the field of decorative
arts.

In general, 19th-century decorative arts demonstrate a high degree of technical skill, and—as
was the case with the printed image—there was a
new ability to mass-produce them. These art
objects reflected the social attitudes of a new
middle-class clientele and allowed novelties that
were produced in many different places to become
more widely known.

Ceramics maintained the traditions of past cen-
turies. France managed to mass-produce ceramics, though with a certain loss of quality. In Sèvres,
paintings were copied on porcelain, and repro-
ductions of Italian Renaissance and Oriental
ceramics were made. Exotic designs were also
popular.

Technical progress in the production of glass
allowed new sizes and shapes to be developed.
(An example can be seen in Paxton's Crystal Palace in London, page 24.) The glass industry in
Venice, Italy, found a new lease on life by copying
ancient designs. France produced ornamental
paperweights, decorated with flowers, insects, or
geometric designs. By the second half of the century, the French were making exquisitely delicate

71

crystal. And in Cartagena, Spain, artists continued to produce glass and white crystal.

Metalworking also flourished during the 19th century, with the development of mass-produced cast iron. There was an increased interest in new uses for iron in monuments and architecture. Decorative grilles for banks and balconies became popular. Stylistically, it was an Eclectic period for metalworking, which combined many elements borrowed from earlier Baroque and Rococo periods.

Working with gold and silver, 19th-century

WILLIAM MORRIS and PHILIP WEBB. *Saint George's Cabinet*. 1862. Victoria and Albert Museum, London.
The statement that Morris could be considered the originator of modern design might appear exag-gerated. After all, the role of the craftsperson was not to resolve all the problems of design in industrial society. But through a company Morris formed, he introduced the idea that all phases of design should be coordinated. Work in stained glass, murals, wallpaper design, metal pieces, furniture, and even jewelry received the attention of specialized artists, who were trying to reestablish what they believed to be the philosophy of integrated craftsmanship.

rench craftspeople made important contribu-
ions to the decorative arts. For example, Charles
Christofle used the newly invented process of
electroplating to make objects for the Vatican as
well as a 1,200-piece set of silver tableware commissioned by Napoleon III.

In the field of textiles, older styles were copied,
generally in an overly ornate fashion. Printed
materials were produced that contained scenes
or large floral patterns. The most interesting innovation in textiles occurred in England, where
William Morris designed materials and wall cov-
erings with an all-over floral pattern.

Despite the enormous spread of mass-
produced books, the art of bookbinding was by
no means lost. Many fanciful, decorative styles
were used and embossed motifs often had a religious theme.

In Spain, the manufacture and use of fans has
long been a strong and special interest. Romantic
fans were large, with highly decorated ribs. Fans
were usually covered with painted or embroi-
dered cloth that depicted all manner of scenes.
Sometimes embossed or engraved paper was also
used as a covering.

By far the most interesting of the century's decorative arts was furniture making. In France, very
ornate furniture—with medieval inspiration—
flourished during the First Restoration. This was
followed during the Second Empire by furniture
designs imitating the styles of the Renaissance
and the reign of Louis XV. In England, Victorian
decoration is synonymous with showiness and
luxury. In both countries, curious items were ini-
tially produced, and they were soon copied all
over Europe. For example, there was the "confi-
dant," an S-shaped seat, and the "indiscreet,"

**LOUIS-ERNEST
BARRIAS.** *Nature
Unveiling Herself before
Science.* 1899. Musée
d'Orsay, Paris.
The use of color is often
ignored by contemporary
art historians studying
19th-century architecture
or sculpture. But studying
the use of color is necessary
to understanding the rest-
lessness of art at the end of
the century. Barrias used
natural colors, integrating
stone of different colors:
marble, onyx, lapis lazuli,
and malachite. Here, he
uses a 19th-century theme
translated into carefully
colored curves that unveil
the taste of a new age.

73

which had a place for a third person. The rocking chair, which originated in America, also became fashionable throughout Europe.

This sampling of the decorative arts demonstrates both the health and the diversity of craft during the 19th century. Nineteenth-century testimony to the value of crafts was witnessed when in 1851, the South Kensington Museum was founded in England. The entire museum was dedicated to the decorative arts. That date can also serve as the starting point of the battle between art and commerce. With the spread of machine-made goods—which were considered inartistic—handcrafted items were seen as the salvation of art and design. William Morris, who established the English Arts and Crafts Movement, was the main defender of this philosophy. In an attempt to eliminate what he considered cheap, mass produced items, he founded a business of his own which designed a wide variety of items, including furniture, wallpaper, jewelry, carpets, and glassware. Morris viewed industrial products as inartistic. He wanted to produce beautiful objects in a society that appeared eager to produce only ugly ones. His actions did not resolve the dilemma of art versus commerce, but they represent a step toward the continuation of well designed and skillfully executed craft items.

GLOSSARY

estheticism: devotion to or emphasis on beauty

cast iron: a type of iron that is cast in a mold and is hard and brittle

classicism: the style of ancient Greece and/or Rome embodied in art, architecture, and literature

droit de seigneur: customary right of a feudal lord to have sexual relations with a tenant's bride on her wedding night

eclecticism: a blending of elements drawn from various sources

fine arts: arts concerned primarily with the the creation of beautiful objects

Gothic: a term used to describe the art and architecture of the Middle Ages (1130-1540)

historicism: a theory that emphasizes the importance of history

iconography: pictorial material that illustrates a subject; the imagery or symbolism in a work of art

impressionism: an art style, begun in France about 1875, that replaced the traditional concept of representation of reality in painting with a new, simpler, pictorial form based on perception and executed through the interplay of light and color; depiction of scenes, characters, or emotions by using details to evoke sensory impressions rather than to create objective reality

Neoclassicism: a movement in art, literature, music, and architecture that revived or adapted Classical style

picturesque: suggesting or resembling a picture or painted scene; charming, quaint, or vivid in appearance

Pre-Raphaelites: members of a brotherhood of artists formed in England in 1848 to restore the artistic practices of Italian art before Raphael

Realism: faithfulness in art to real life; the accurate representation of objects without idealizing them; a concern for fact or reality and rejection of the visionary

Romanticism: a literary and artistic movement that originated in the 18th century. It was characterized primarily by a rejection of Neoclassicism and an emphasis on the imagination and emotions.

subjectivity: an artist's individual view

Symbolism: an artistic movement in which objects are invested with symbolic meaning, and intangible or immaterial truths are expressed in terms of visible representation, or symbols

terra-cotta: a brownish orange clay used for statues, vases, and architectural purposes

ART THROUGHOUT THE AGES

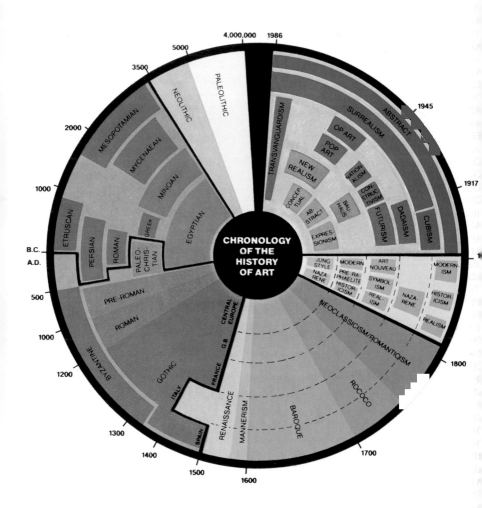

CHRONOLOGY OF THE HISTORY OF ART

This chart shows the evolution of Western and Near Eastern art through the ages. The terms are those that art historians traditionally use to label periods of time in various cultures where definite stylistic tendencies have occurred. The books in the Key to Art series examine the interplay of artists, ideas, methods, and cultural influences that have affected the evolution of specific art styles.

INDEX OF ILLUSTRATIONS

CONTENTS

Acknowledgments
Aisa: p. 47; A.K.G., Berlin: p. 30; A.P.: pp. 7, 15, 16 (top), 22, 24, 25, 26, 27, 33, 41, 49, 50-51, 54, 55, 47, 58, 64, 65, 66, 67, 69, 70; Bridgeman-Index: pp. 9, 72; Bulloz: p. 61; Giraudon: pp. 10, 31, 32, 36, 43, 45, 47, 59, 73; I.G.D.A.: pp. 5, 6, 11, 12, 20, 41 (bottom), 42, 48 (top), 52, 53, 56, 63, 71; I.M.H., Barcelona: p. 17; National Gallery, London: p. 44; Oronoz: pp. 3, 8 (top), 13, 14, 21, 23, 28, 34, 35, 37, 40, 46, 50, 60; Sammlung Georg Shäfer, Euerbach: p. 38